s u s h i

sushi

RYUICHI YOSHII

PERIPLUS

contents

s u s h i

The Japanese believe that food should satisfy all the senses. Food is always prepared with great care and beautifully presented: sometimes very simply, and sometimes in an intricate array. The freshest ingredients are combined in ways that delight the eyes as well as the taste buds. Seasonings are generally quite subtle, in order to enhance the natural flavors.

Sushi combines seasonal seafood and rice, the staple diet of the Japanese people. A wide variety of vegetables can be used in sushi, too. There are more sushi restaurants in Japan than any other type of restaurant, although traditional sushi shops are becoming rare. The increasing number of sushi restaurants outside Japan attests to the worldwide popularity of this delightfully appetizing food.

Because of extensive fishing, refrigerated transport and extremely efficient distribution, no matter where you live in Japan you can eat fresh fish daily, both from Japanese waters and from overseas.

Sashimi means "raw" in Japanese and is generally used to refer to the delicately arranged plates of raw seafood and sliced fresh fish that are served with soy and other dipping sauces. *Sushi* refers to vinegar-flavored rice topped with sashimi, omelettes and vegetables, or rolled with a variety of fillings in dark green nori seaweed.

Sashimi is usually served as an entree, and sushi as a main course or as the penultimate dish in a Japanese dinner, prior to dessert. Miso soup may be served with sushi.

There is an enormous variety of sushi. The ingredients are almost limitless and there are many different ways of making sushi, from traditional forms in which rice and fish are packed together in a container and fermented over a period of time to the most incredible decorative sushi featuring patterns, birds, flowers, fruits and figures. Modern sushi bars most commonly serve maki-zushi, which are bite-sized rolls of sushi rice and seafood or vegetables wrapped in nori seaweed, and nigiri-zushi, which consist of slivers of raw fish or other ingredients laid over bite-sized "bricks" of sushi rice. (Sushi is pronounced "zushi" when it follows a vowel.)

Making sushi is both easy enough to be done at home and so complicated that it takes years for the professional chef to master. If you are a beginner, the recipes for chirashi-zushi and temaki-zushi given in this book may be the easiest to follow initially. Chirashi-zushi is sushi rice and other ingredients served in a bowl; temaki-zushi is hand-rolled cones of nori seaweed (rolled like ice-cream cones) containing sushi rice and various fillings. With some basic equipment, you should have little trouble mastering maki-zushi and, when you are ready for a challenge, you can move on to nigiri-zushi. To make maki-zushi and nigiri-zushi you will need to invest in some of the cooking utensils that are recommended on pages 12–15.

Sushi is a simple, light and healthy food. Raw fish and seafood contain many vitamins and minerals, a high amount of health-giving omega-3 fatty acids and little cholesterol.

Right: Tuna, squid and salmon nigiri-zushi
(see pages 34 and 72–3)

Sushi chefs

Training for sushi chefs is traditionally long and hard. An apprentice spends much of his time with his hands in cold water, doing chores in the kitchen. An apprentice may start training as young as 15 years old and spend the first two years learning to make sushi rice, which in itself requires considerable skill. He will then move on to learning the art of preparing fish, and finally he will actually make sushi.

Until recently, sushi masters were little interested in having students, perhaps because of the potential competition. Often, when the apprentice came to work, the sushi chef would just use him to carry fish home from the market and then as a delivery boy, so the apprentice was never in the bar when sushi were being prepared. A bright apprentice would soon realize what was going on and would have to insist that the sushi chef show him the wide range of skills he needed to acquire.

A trainee learns to be a sushi chef by carefully watching his master at work and then by repeatedly experimenting himself. Eventually, when the apprentice has fully mastered the intricacies of sushi making, he may either work alongside his master or go into business and set up his own sushi bar.

A good sushi chef, in addition to having mastered the standard sushi repertoire, will also be an creative artist. He will be able to create an extensive range of decorative sushi and sashimi in fanciful forms, which may be served on special occasions or for festivals.

Eating sushi at a sushi bar

At a sushi bar, you can order your food from a menu or choose items from the refrigerated glass case in front of you. Often, it is best to rely on the sushi chef's advice. The selection of fish at the markets varies from day to day, and as he will have selected the fish himself the sushi chef will be able to recommend the freshest and best sushi to you, and serve them in the most appropriate order. You may wish to start your meal with sashimi and have a bowl of miso soup with your sushi.

On the plate with the sushi, you will be given a small heap of wasabi, a spicy condiment, and a small heap of slices of pickled ginger (gari). Served alongside will be a small bowl of soy sauce. With your meal, it is traditional to drink tea. Japanese tea is generally called *ocha*. When drunk with sushi it is called *agari*.

Sushi is often served with decorations made from bamboo or aspidistra leaves, and at some sushi bars leaves are used instead of plates. The leaf decorations serve a practical purpose in separating sushi pieces and are a means of demonstrating the chef's cutting skills.

When eating nigiri-zushi, it is traditional to use your hands and then wipe them on a towel. You may also use chopsticks. Take a dab of wasabi on your chopstick, gently pick up a piece of sushi and dip the end of the topping in the bowl of soy sauce. Do not dip the rice side of the sushi in the soy as you will simply taste soy, rather than the flavors of both rice and topping. Put the sushi in your mouth with the topping side down—so the fish meets your taste buds. (Do not mix the wasabi in the soy sauce, as you will drown the sushi with the flavor of the wasabi.)

Maki-zushi can be eaten either with your hand or with chopsticks, picking the roll up at the sides.

After eating a piece of sushi, eat a slice of pickled ginger to clean your palate, have a sip of tea, then eat the next sushi. Japanese green tea removes oiliness after eating fish and prepares the palate for the next piece. Sushi bars serve tea that has a slightly bitter flavor—sweet tea should be avoided as it diminishes the flavor of the sushi.

Nowadays, people drink beer, wine or sake with sushi. Sake, the traditional Japanese drink made from fermented

Right: Temaki-zushi (see pages 68–9)

rice, comes in a variety of styles. It varies from dry to sweet, like wine, and may be drunk chilled or hot. For sushi, try subtle styles of sake which will not overpower the fresh tastes. Delicately flavored white wines will also balance well with sushi, enhancing and complementing the flavors.

When you receive your bill, do not be too shocked at the total. The best sushi bars sell only the highest quality fresh fish, which is becoming increasingly expensive.

The origins of sushi

The earliest sushi methods probably came to Japan from Southeast Asia or China, at about the time that the Japanese were learning to grow rice. As early as 500 B.C., the mountain people in Thailand, Laos and North Borneo used river fish and rice in pickling and fermenting processes that preserved the fish. A similar fermenting process was used in China in early times, but through the reign of Mongolia over China (1368–1644) the process was lost, perhaps because Mongolians do not eat seafood.

In Japan, sushi was seen originally as a way of preserving fish. Layers of carp and layers of rice were placed in a jar with a lid on top and left to ferment for up to a year. The fish would be eaten and the rice thrown away. As time went by, methods of fermentation were developed that took only a few days, so the rice, which had a sharp, sweet taste, could be eaten as well as the fish. (In Shiga Prefecture today, the traditional fermentation process for carp and rice, known as nare-zushi, is still used.)

Several centuries ago, the people of Tokyo (or Edo as it was then called) were known for their businesslike impatience. In the 1640s, they came up with the idea of adding vinegar to the rice to give it a fermented flavor without the bother of having to wait a few days for fermentation to take place.

In early sushi making, the fish was either marinated, boiled in soy and mirin, or grilled. In time, the range expanded to include raw fish—sashimi. In the early 1800s, a man called Yohei Hanaya began serving sashimi on sushi rice at his street stall, or yattai, in Tokyo, which marks the beginning of the current style of nigiri-zushi. He brought his fish to his stall in an icebox, which he would then open to show his customers the day's selection.

This yattai stall was a wagon with a counter, and it had a curtain. Until early this century, the most popular sushi stalls were those that had the dirtiest curtains: A dirty curtain meant a busy shop, and therefore a good one. Customers would eat their sushi, dip their fingers in their tea and then wipe their hands on the curtain to dry them. Sushi bar tea cups are large, so they can double as finger bowls. Since the 1950s, sushi has moved indoors to more Western-style, seated establishments. (Even though they no longer serve sushi, you can still visit yattai stalls for cheap outdoor meals in some parts of Japan, particularly in Kyushu.)

Oshi-zushi is a style of sushi making that evolved in Osaka. To make oshi-zushi, fresh seafood or other ingredients are placed in a custom-made wooden box, sushi rice is added, and then a lid is put on to press the sushi together to form a cube. The cube is cut into bite-sized pieces for serving.

As a result of both geography and history, there are many regional differences in Japanese cuisine. Broadly speaking, food prepared in the Kanto region, which includes Tokyo and Yokohama, differs from the Kansai style of Osaka, Kyoto and thereabouts. Kansai-style cooking is seen as "haute cuisine," with subtle flavors, whereas Kanto flavors tend to be stronger, using stronger miso and more soy sauce. Chefs will generally have a preference for one or the other style.

Right: (Clockwise from back) Salmon rose, Thin-omelette, and Squid nigiri-zushi (see pages 38 and 72–3)

The following items are recommended for making sushi and are obtainable from Japanese specialty stores and some larger Asian supermarkets. In many cases, you will find that substitutes from your kitchen cupboards are suitable. For making sushi rolls, a bamboo rolling mat is essential, and if you have tweezers, a fish scaler and high-quality knives you will find handling and filleting fish a great deal easier.

Bamboo rolling mat (makisu)

The simple rolling mat used for making sushi rolls is made of thin strips of bamboo woven with cotton string. After you have used the mat, scrub it down with a brush and dry it thoroughly, otherwise it may become moldy. It is best to buy an all-purpose mat measuring 12 x 12 inches (30 x 30 cm), but smaller ones are also available. When making sushi, the mat must be dry.

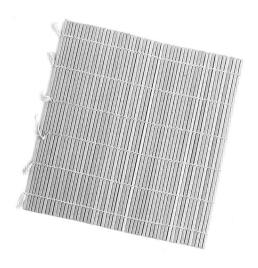

Bamboo rolling mat (makisu)

Bowl with lid

A large bowl with a lid is needed for holding the cooked sushi rice once it has been prepared, to keep it warm. An insulated bowl is ideal.

Chopping board

A chopping board is needed for a variety of tasks, from preparing fish and vegetables to assembling all the different sorts of sushi. A wooden chopping board always used to be used for sushi making, but now resin boards are widely available and are easier to keep free of odors.

It is best to have a board measuring at least 10 inches x 15 inches (25 cm x 38 cm).

Chopsticks (saibashi)

The chopsticks used for cooking are two to three times longer than chopsticks used for eating. Cooking chopsticks are extremely useful implements, once you have mastered the technique, as they enable you to manipulate food using only one hand. You will also probably want to have several pairs of chopsticks for individual use when serving sushi and sashimi.

Cooking chopsticks

Fan (uchiwa)

An uchiwa is a flat fan made of paper or silk stretched over light bamboo ribs, and is traditionally used for cooling and separating the sushi rice. While it is delightful to own an uchiwa, a piece of heavy paper or cardboard will do the job just as well.

Fish scaler

When cleaning and preparing fish at home, it is easiest to use a scaler, available from a fish market. Simply draw it up the body of the fish, working from tail to head. Do not use the back of a cleaver as a substitute, as you run the risk of bruising the fish.

Flat grater

Fish scaler

Grater

Sushi chefs use a length of sharkskin for grating wasabi root; for grating pieces of ginger and daikon, they use a ceramic bowl that has small teeth on the surface.

If you are using a straightforward household grater, a flat one made of stainless steel is most suitable. Be sure to choose one that is comfortable to hold and has closely packed, sharp teeth. When using the grater, particularly when grating ginger, use a circular motion.

Knives

Japanese chefs use knives that are traditionally made from the same steel that was used to make samurai swords. They are renowned for their strength and sharpness.

The best sort of knife to use for filleting fish and for slicing pieces of fish for sashimi and sushi is a long, slender one with a pointed end. A wide, heavy knife is useful for cutting through bone, as when removing a fish's head. Never use a serrated knife when cutting fish, as it will tear the flesh, spoiling its appearance.

For chopping and slicing vegetables, a long, square-ended cleaver is most suitable.

Sharp, strong, good-quality steel knives are needed for the best results. Look after your knives and either sharpen them on a whetstone or have them sharpened by a professional. Sushi chefs keep a damp cloth nearby, to wipe the knives clean from time to time while they work.

Mixing bowls

You will need several mixing bowls. Stainless steel ones are recommended.

Plates for sushi

When serving sushi, you need a set of plates that are as flat as possible. If the rim of a serving plate is curved or ridged, as is common with Western-style crockery, the presentation of the sushi will not be as attractive and they will probably fall over.

Rice-cooling tub (hangiri)

The broad, wooden hangiri, generally made of cypress, and with low sides, is designed specifically for cooling sushi rice. This gives the rice the ideal texture and gloss, but a nonmetallic flat-bottomed bowl can be substituted instead. The bigger the bowl the better, as you will then be able to stir and separate the rice grains properly.

If you are using a hangiri, wash it well after use, dry it carefully, then wrap it in a cloth and store it face downward in a cool, dry place.

Heavy chopping knife and long, thin filleting knife

Rice-cooling tub (hangiri) and wooden rice paddle (shamoji)

Rice maker

An electric or gas rice maker is highly recommended for cooking rice, as it will control the temperature and cooking time to give perfect rice every time. Otherwise, you can use a heavy pot with a tight-fitting lid.

Skewers

When cooking shrimp, it is best to use either bamboo skewers or long toothpicks.

Stainless-steel colander

A colander is used for straining rice and for washing and draining other ingredients.

Square omelette pan

A square-shaped omelette pan about 1 inch (3 cm) deep is traditionally used for making sushi omelettes. A thick pan that retains heat is ideal, but can be heavy to handle. You can substitute a conventional round skillet about 10 inches (25 cm) in diameter and trim the sides of the omelette once it has been cooked to make it square.

Tweezers

Heavy, straight-ended tweezers come in handy for deboning fish. These are obtainable from a fish market.

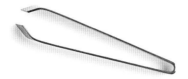

Tweezers for deboning fish

Wooden rice paddle (shamoji)

A wooden rice paddle, called a shamoji, is traditionally used for turning and spreading sushi rice when cooling it, but any kind of broad, flat utensil will do the job. You can use a large wooden spoon or a wooden spatula. Because wood tends to absorb flavors, it is best to use your chosen spoon exclusively for sushi rice.

Before using a wooden spoon for sushi rice, wet it thoroughly, or the rice will stick to it.

Square omelette pan

Japanese people, on the whole, love to live in harmony with nature and therefore favor eating fresh foods in season. In keeping with this attitude, and for the best results, use the freshest foods possible when making sushi.

The range of possible ingredients for sushi is vast, limited only by what is available and the cook's imagination. This list features ingredients used in the recipes that follow, including certain forms of preserved fish. Fresh fish and seafood are covered separately in the next chapter. There are, of course, many traditional ingredients, some of which may be new to you, but they will generally be obtainable from Asian food stores and the larger supermarkets.

Traditionally, sushi has been largely fish-based, but ingredients other than fish and seafood are becoming increasingly popular. Tofu is a recent arrival in the repertoire, as are snow pea sprouts and other types of sprout. When selecting vegetables for sushi, go to the best-quality store in your neighborhood and choose only the freshest, firmest produce, as generally it is served either raw or blanched.

Japanese ingredients are highly recommended—soy sauce, sake, sushi vinegar and other seasonings—as they are made traditionally to suit Japanese foods. Substituting other ingredients will result in different flavors.

Right: Some of the vegetables used in sushi include asparagus, snow peas (mange-touts), avocado, eggplant and ginger

Bonito flakes

Avocado

Use avocados that are ripe but firm. The best ones for sushi have a thin, smooth skin and green and gold flesh. Before being used for sushi, avocados are thinly sliced.

Bonito flakes (katsuo boshi)

These sandy brown flakes of smoked, dried and fermented bonito fish are used to make dashi, which is a basic Japanese stock. For household use, instant dashi (hon-dashi) can be used—granules of bonito that are simply added to water to make stock.

Carrots

Select carrots that are crisp and bright orange. Cut into lengths of 2–4 inches (5–10 cm) before slicing. Carrots can be made into the most intricate decorations to accompany sushi and sashimi (see page 40).

Aji-ponzu

A yellow-colored vinegar that tastes particularly good with salmon. Ponzu is the name of a lemon and soy dipping sauce that can be bought ready-made.

Aka oroshi

Japanese red chili paste. This is mixed with grated daikon radish and used as a garnish for white-fish sushi. Do not substitute other types of chili paste, as they will probably be too pungent.

Asparagus

Choose asparagus with straight stalks and good color. Blanch in salted, boiling water and cut into 2–4 inch (5 cm–10 cm) lengths before using, and cut them lengthwise into several slices if they are thick.

Carrot and cucumber decorations

Daikon radish

Chili seasonings

See aka oroshi. Ichimi togarashi is mild Japanese chili powder. Do not use other forms of chili paste or powder as substitutes, as they will probably be too strong.

Chives

This herb is used in 1-inch (2.5-cm) slices in sashimi rolls and is minced to garnish white-fish sushi.

Cucumber

Japanese cucumbers are about 6–8 inches (15–20 cm) long. They are less watery than American cucumbers and have fewer seeds, firmer insides and softer skins. If you can't find Japanese cucumbers, use a 6–8 inch (15–20 cm) piece of European (hothouse) cucumber. Buy firm-skinned cucumbers

with a medium green color. Cut into 2–4 inch (5–10 cm) lengths before slicing. Cucumber is often used as a filling in sushi rolls and is cut into decorations to ornament sashimi and sushi plates (see page 40).

Daikon radish

A Japanese giant white radish with a smooth skin, at least 20 in (50 cm) long. Daikon is less pungent than many radishes. Look for firm, shiny ones with smooth skin and straight leaves. Peel them deep enough to remove both the skin and fibers beneath it. Cut into 2–4 inch (5–10 cm) lengths before slicing.

Daikon contains various enzymes and is good for the digestion when eating strongly flavored oily foods. Cut into fine slivers, it is eaten with sashimi; paper-thin slices are rolled around sashimi in the place of nori seaweed; and grated daikon is added to soy sauce and other sauces for texture and flavor.

Eel

Fresh eel is not widely available: much of it worldwide is exported to Japan where it is made into unagi—eel prepared in the Japanese manner. Unagi is steamed and then broiled, after being brushed with soy sauce and mirin. You can buy frozen unagi eel at Asian supermarkets.

Eggplant (aubergine)

Japanese eggplants are similar to Chinese eggplants, which are smaller and thinner than Italian (globe) eggplants. They are usually 6–8 inches (15–20 cm) long and about 2 inches (5 cm) in diameter. Choose firm, purple, smooth-fleshed ones with straight stalks. If using larger eggplant, peel off the skin. Eggplant should be sliced, then lightly grilled or fried before being used in sushi.

Enoki mushrooms

These white mushrooms have long, thin stalks and tiny caps. Choose ones that are crisp and white: Yellowish brown ones are old and should be avoided. Cut off the "roots" at the bottom of the stalks.

Gari

Ginger slices that have been pickled in salt and sweet vinegar. They are a delicate pink color and are available in bottles and other forms of packaging. The bright red vinegared ginger is not used with sushi. Small amounts of gari are eaten between bites of sushi to freshen the palate.

Ginger

The thick, rootlike rhizome of the ginger plant has a sharp, pungent flavor. Ginger should be firm, with a smooth skin. Once the thin, tan skin is peeled away from fresh ginger, the

Gari (pickled ginger slices)

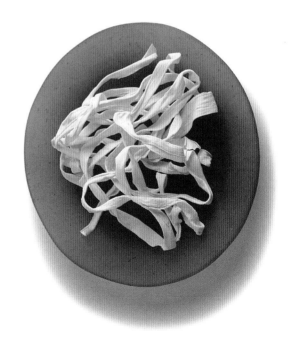

Fresh ginger

Dried kampyo

Cooked kampyo

flesh is sliced or grated. Store fresh ginger in the refrigerator. Grated ginger is used to garnish white-fish sushi. *See also* gari.

Kamaboko

Japanese-style fish cakes, available frozen. There are various forms, some of them dyed pink. Kamaboko can be used in chirashi-zushi (see page 94).

Kampyo

Dried bottle gourd or calabash, used in the form of shavings or ribbonlike strips. Before being used in sushi, kampyo is tenderized and seasoned (see page 96 for method).

Kimchee

Korean spicy fermented cabbage. Kimchee is strongly flavored, so use only a small quantity.

Kombu

Dried kelp. This sea vegetable is available in the form of hard, flat, black sheets that have a fine white powder on the surface. Kombu is used to flavor dashi, a basic soup stock, and sushi rice. Wipe the surface of the sheets with a damp cloth before use to remove the powder: do not wash the kombu as you will diminish its flavor. Avoid kombu that is wrinkled and thin.

Lotus root (renkon)

The crunchy root of the lotus plant is used in a variety of Japanese dishes, including chirashi-zushi. It is peeled, then sliced before cooking. The slices resemble white wheels with holes in them. It discolors as soon as it is cut, so place slices in water to which 1 teaspoon vinegar has been added. It is hard to find fresh lotus root, but vinegared lotus root is available in packets.

Mayonnaise

Mayonnaise goes well with certain sushi, but be sure to use either homemade egg mayonnaise or commercially available mild-flavored creamy egg mayonnaise. It can be mixed with soy sauce as a garnish for California rolls.

Mirin

Sweet alcoholic wine made from rice. Store in a cool, dark place after opening. If mirin is unavailable, use 1 teaspoon sugar in place of 1 tablespoon mirin.

Mirin (left) and soy sauce (right)

Natto

Miso

A fermented mixture of soybeans, salt and water and a fermenting agent—usually soy "koji," rice or barley. There are many types and mixtures of miso, but they can be broadly divided into three categories: sweet, nonsweet and salty.

White miso, the sweetest, is ivory to yellow in color and is seldom available outside Japan. What is commonly known as white miso is golden colored and has a mild flavor. Red miso is aged the longest and is the salty form; it is actually dark brown. White and red miso, plus many blends, are available in Asian supermarkets.

Natto

Fermented soybeans. Natto has a rich flavor, similar to cheese, a pungent odor and a rather glutinous consistency. Many Japanese enjoy natto for breakfast.

Nori

Sheets of seaweed used for making rolls. The sheets measure about $7^{1}/_{2}$ x 8 inches (19 x 20.5 cm) and are sold in cellophane or plastic bags. Once the wrapping has been opened, use the nori as soon as possible or store it in a container in a cool place.

Make sure you buy precooked nori, known as yaki-nori, which is dark green. The black or purple types of nori are raw and must be toasted over a flame.

Ocha

Japanese tea. The kind served with Japanese meals is generally green tea. Bancha and sencha are types of green tea, and are available in leaf and powdered form or in teabags. Bancha should steep for 2–3 minutes; sencha should steep for 1 minute only. Gyokuro and other expensive green teas are not suitable for serving with sushi. When served with sushi, ocha is known as agari.

Nori

Sake

Japanese fermented rice wine. Sake is used in cooking to tenderize meat and fish, and to make ingredients more flavorful. It also counteracts acidity. Buy cooking sake (ryori sake) or inexpensive drinking sake for making sushi.

Salt

Rock salt or sea salt is best.

Scallions (shallots/spring onions)

Buy thin, straight, moist shoots that are firm and crisp. The Japanese use most of the green part of scallions, discarding only the very tip. Chopped scallions are used as a garnish with white-fish sushi and in miso soup.

Okra

This vegetable, sometimes known as gumbo, comes in the form of five-sided pods that taper to a point, with a flowerlike cross-section filled with seeds. Choose crisp, young okra, 2–4 inches (5–10 cm) long. It keeps for 2 or 3 days in the refrigerator, loosely wrapped in plastic. Okra is boiled, then cut in half lengthwise for use in sushi.

Rice

Short-grain white rice. Use Japanese rice or California short-grain rice. The size, consistency, taste and smell of other types of rice are not suitable for making sushi.

Short-grain white rice

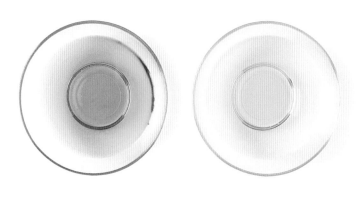

Rice vinegar and sake

Dried shiitake mushrooms

Sesame seeds (goma)

White sesame seeds are most commonly used. You can buy them toasted or toast them yourself in a pan over medium heat, moving them around so that they turn golden brown and do not burn. Black sesame seeds are used as a garnish for cuttlefish and are sometimes used for sushi decoration.

Shiitake mushrooms

When buying fresh shiitake mushrooms, choose plump-looking ones with dark brown caps, cleanly tucked edges and white coloring underneath. For use in sushi, shiitake mushrooms may be parboiled, but taste better if they have been lightly grilled. To prepare shiitake mushrooms, use a knife to score an asterisk pattern on the caps, but avoid cutting through the flesh. This ensures even cooking and looks decorative.

Fresh shiitake mushrooms

If using dried shiitake mushrooms, choose brown-capped ones that have been well dried and are therefore cracked-looking. Soak them in water for at least 30 minutes before using. The longer they are soaked, the softer they become. When soaked, good-quality shiitake mushrooms are fleshy and plump.

Shiso

This aromatic herb, a member of the mint family, is known in the West as perilla. Buy fresh, green leaves. There is also a red variety that is used for coloring and flavoring umeboshi and other Japanese pickles.

Snow peas (mange-touts)

These should be bright green, and should still be crisp after blanching. Blanch in salted, boiling water beforeusing.

Snow pea sprouts

Available from produce vegetable stores, snow pea sprouts are sold in packets that prevent them being crushed and keep them fresh.

Soboro

A pink ingredient made from white fish, used in chirashi-zushi. You can buy it ready-made, in a jar.

Soy sauce (shoyu)

A salty sauce made from soybeans and used both as an ingredient and as a table condiment. Dark soy sauce is thicker and often less salty than light soy sauce. Low-sodium products are also available. Japanese soy is more suitable for sushi, as it is naturally fermented and less salty than Chinese soy.

Sushi vinegar (awasezu)

Sushi vinegar is a mild-tasting vinegar made from rice, as are other Japanese vinegars. It is specifically made for sushi. Other vinegars cannot be substituted, as they are too strong.

Shiso

Tofu

Tofu

A white curd of custardlike texture made from soybean milk. Use the Japanese "silken" variety, which has a soft, glossy surface and a melt-in-your-mouth texture. Japanese tofu is softer and smoother than Chinese tofu. Once opened, tofu must be kept in the refrigerator, in water deep enough to cover it. Change the water at least twice a day. Stored this way, tofu will last 2 days.

Slices of deep-fried tofu, known as abura-age-dofu, are used to make pouches that are stuffed with sushi rice, known as inari-zushi (see page 90).

Tofu is widely available; abura-age can be found in Asian supermarkets.

Umeboshi

Salty pickled plums. These are available in bottles and in paste form. Keep opened bottles in the refrigerator.

Vinegar *See* sushi vinegar.

Umeboshi

Wakame

A type of seaweed available in dried form, reconstituted under running water, used to flavor miso soup.

Wakame seaweed

Wasabi

Japanese horseradish. Wasabi roots are olive green with a bumpy skin. The best roots are 4–5 years old, 4–6 inches (10–15 cm) long and should be fat and moist.

Fresh wasabi is expensive and largely unavailable outside Japan, so powdered or paste formulations are commonly used. The powder, which is mixed with a small amount of tepid water to make a paste, is the more economical of the two. You can sometimes buy frozen grated wasabi, or you can mix Western horseradish with wasabi powder. When served as an accompaniment to sushi, wasabi is sometimes made into a decorative shape, such as a leaf.

When making wasabi paste from powdered wasabi, prepare only a small quantity at a time as its potency diminishes quickly.

Wasabi

seafood

Buy the freshest fish possible for making sashimi and sushi, for reasons of health, taste and beauty. If you can, go to the fish markets, and always buy fish and seafood in season. Most fish can be eaten raw, but it is best to use fish that are commonly used in sashimi and sushi. Fish and seafood should be kept refrigerated until needed.

Selecting whole fish

Whenever possible, buy fish whole and fillet them at home. You can then be sure that the meat is fresh. Use the following guidelines to ensure that whole fish are fresh.

- Check that the eyes are plump, clear and bright. Avoid fish with cloudy pupils.

- The gills should be bright pink-red and look moist. If fish is not fresh, the gills are black-red.

- Overall, the coloring of the fish should be bright or lustrous.

- Stroke the fish to ensure that the flesh is firm and elastic. Stale fish are less elastic and may feel sticky.

- The fish should have a "clean" smell. Avoid ones that have a strong fishy odor.

- Mackerel should have a pointed shape to their stomachs, and the tail on both mackerel and bonito should be upright. A drooping tail shows that a fish is not fresh.

Selecting portions of fish

With bigger fish, it may be inconvenient or uneconomical to buy a whole fish, so buy fillets and smaller cuts. When buying only a portion of a fish, use the following guidelines.

- Fillets should be moist and have a good color.

- White fish should look almost transparent.

- Cut tuna flesh should have distinct stripes in it around the belly and be clear red without stripes in other parts.

- The head end of fish is more tender than the tail end.

- With most fish, the back is the most delicious part. Tuna and swordfish are exceptions, in that the tender, fatty belly area is most sought-after.

Selecting seafood

- When buying shrimp, if they are alive they should be active and of good color. If they are no longer alive, check that the stripes are distinct: they should not be blurred together.

- Touch the tentacles of squid and check that the suckers are still active. The skin around the eyes should be clear blue.

- Sea urchins should be yellow or orange, firm and not slimy.

- Live shellfish are best. When you gently open the shell, it should close by itself.

Right: Fresh, raw tuna

When to buy fish in season

Australia and New Zealand

Winter: silver dory, ling, gemfish, mackerel, Pacific and angasi oysters, tuna, cod

Spring: salmon, shrimp (prawns), lobster, crabs, Murray cod, yabbies, golden trout

Summer: swordfish, yellowfin tuna, red emperor, mud crab, Sydney rock oysters, harbour prawns, reef fish

Autumn: whiting, garfish, blue-eye cod, mackerel, tuna, broadbill snapper

United States

Winter: herring, littleneck clam, Maine sea urchin, sweet shrimp

Spring: ark shell, bonito, fluke, horse mackerel, porgy, Maine sea urchin, smelt, soft-shell crab, spear squid

Summer: ark shell, blue abalone, blue-fin crab, Boston tuna, mackerel, Meiji tuna, red abalone, porgy, sea bass, California sea urchin, striped bass

Autumn: Boston tuna, mackerel, sea bass, California sea urchin

Preparing fish and seafood

Before cutting the fish, rinse and wipe your cutting board.

Either keep a bowl of water beside you to wet your knife and then wipe it, or wipe the knife occasionally with a clean, damp cloth.

There are various methods for cutting different types of fish. The most common of these is the three-part method, or san-mai oroshi style. This is used for most fish, apart from larger flatfish and very large fish.

If you have problems holding the fish, or the bones are scratching you, use a clean kitchen glove on the hand that is holding the fish.

Try not to handle the body of the fish too much as you may cause bruising. Hold the fish by its head or tail whenever possible.

Three-part method for filleting fish
(san-mai oroshi style)

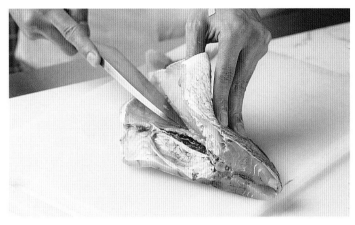

1. Thoroughly wash the fish and scale it, if scaling is required. Lay the fish down on the board. Use a sharp knife to chop off the head, cutting from under the gills to the top of the head. Cut off the fins on the back and stomach side and hard flaps near the head.

2. With the fish on its side, use your knife to make an incision in the fish belly (only as far as the spine) and slice along the belly side of fish from the head to the anal orifice. With your hands, remove the viscera and, with your knife skimming along the spine, remove the fish stomach. Wash the visceral cavity under running water and then use a brush to scrape off any blood.

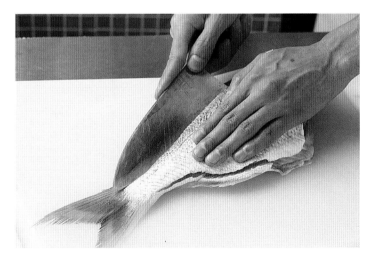

3. Put the fish on the board again, and now cut along the back of the fish from the tail to the (missing) head, with your knife tip just running along the edge of the spine.

4. Now let the knife go all the way through, and run it along the length of the fish and lift off the fillet.

6. Any remaining bones in the fillets or around the visceral area should be plucked or trimmed away.

5. Turn the fish over and then slice along the fish back from head to tail, skimming along the spine.

Slice along the belly side from tail to head, letting the knife go all the way through to cut the second fillet.

7. You now have three parts: two fillets and one piece consisting of the skeleton and the tail.

Skinning a fillet of fish

Fish such as mackerel, bonito, sea bream and garfish may be eaten with their skin on. Salmon, tuna, swordfish and cod are usually skinned. To skin a fillet:

1. Lay the fillet on the board, skin-side down.

2. Holding the tail end with your left hand, insert the blade of your knife carefully between the skin and flesh at the tail end.

3. Using your left hand to add pressure and to hold onto the fish skin at the tail end, slowly pull the skin and flesh, keeping the knife at an angle without moving it and gently let the knife run along the length of the fillet from tail to head, just skimming along the skin.

4. As you work, use the side of the knife to push or roll the flesh away as you remove the skin.

For both sashimi and sushi, fish fillets should be deboned, scaled and, where necessary, skinned. The parts of the fish that are not usable for sashimi and sushi may be used in many other ways. The spine can be used for making stock, and the scraps that are not suitable for sashimi or nigiri-zushi may be used for rolled sushi, or may be minced or added to soups or other recipes.

You will generally need to cut fish fillets into workable-sized blocks before making sashimi and sushi. The length will depend on the fish being used, but the block should be rectangular in shape, measuring about 3 inches (7 cm) across and $1^{1}/_{2}$ inches (4 cm) high. Slices should be $^{1}/_{4}$–$^{1}/_{2}$ inch (0.5–1 cm) thick. Remember that the slices and resulting sushi should be bite-sized.

Cleaning squid

1. Holding the body part in one hand, use the other hand to pull the tentacles away.

2. Reach inside the body cavity and remove the remaining parts, including the quill.

3. Insert a finger under the fin to separate, and then pull off the fin and as much skin as possible.

4. Peel off the remaining skin.

5. Use a knife to cut off the tentacles above the eyes. The tentacles may be used in other dishes.

6. Thoroughly wash the body inside and out.

Sushi and sashimi cutting

When cutting fish for sushi and sashimi, always cut with the knife pulling the slice toward you. The flesh should be sliced on the bias along the length of the fish or the fillet to give the best results texturally, visually and for taste.

For sashimi, there are some basic cutting techniques: a straight-down cut, an angled cut (also used for sushi), a cubic cut (for tuna), a flat cut that is then cut into fine threadlike strips, and a paper-thin-slice cut.

Any fish can be cut in these styles and eaten as sashimi, or these basic techniques can be used as a foundation for more decorative sashimi.

Angled cut for sushi and sashimi (sorigiri)

To slice fish for sushi topping, the ideal is to start with a rectangular block of fish about the width of your hand, measuring about 3 inches (7 cm) across and 1¹/2 inches (4 cm) high.

With a large fish, such as tuna, you would be able to cut a block like this from the larger block that you had bought. With other fish, such as salmon, try to cut the fish into a block, although the ends and sides may not be particularly even. With salmon or white fish, you can often cut following the existing angle of the fillet.

Measure about 1¹/2 inches (4 cm) in from the top and slice off a triangular piece to make an angled edge to work with. (Any scraps can be used in rolled sushi.)

With your knife on a slant to match the angle of the working edge of the block, cut slices about ¹/4–¹/2 inch (6 mm–1 cm) thick. The remaining piece of the block will also be triangular.

This method is also used with smaller filleted fish, adjusting the knife angle to suit the fillet. With fish such as tuna, the resulting slices will be uniform and rectangular. With smaller fillets, you may have triangular edges or thinner slices. Sometimes you may need to use more than one slice for a piece of nigiri-zushi.

This angled cut is used to slice raw fish such as tuna or salmon for sushi and sashimi

Sashimi cuts

Straight cut: Using a squared-off edge of filleted fish, cut ¹/₄-inch (6-mm) slices straight down along the fish. With tuna, the slices need to be a little thicker than for some other fish because the flesh is likely to break up along the lines if the slices are thin.

Cubic cut for tuna: Slice straight down through the fish, making ¹/₂–1-inch (12 mm–2.5-cm) thick slices, then cut the slices into cubes of the same width.

Fine-strip cut for white fish or squid: Cut ¹/₄ inch (¹/₂ cm) straight slices from the fillet. Lay each slice flat and cut them lengthwise into strips ¹/₂ inch (6 mm) wide.

Paper-thin slicing for white fish: Measure about 1¹/₂ inches (4 cm) in from the top of the block of fish and slice off a triangular piece to make an angled edge to work with. Steadily use your knife to cut paper-thin slices at an angle along the fish.

With many white fish, the resulting slices are almost transparent.

Straight cut used to slice raw fish for sashimi

Straight-down cut and angled cut

A wide variety of fish and seafood can be enjoyed as sashimi, allowing you to experience the full, natural flavor and texture of fish in season. *Sashimi* means "raw" in Japanese.

Sashimi is sliced and prepared in various ways, depending on the texture of the ingredient being used, and then decoratively presented. Sashimi is usually eaten at the beginning of a meal, as a light appetizer. Various dipping sauces and accompaniments are used to enhance the flavors of the fish.

There is a very old tradition in Japan of always serving sashimi with an odd number of slices, as on the facing page. We do not know how this tradition arose.

White fish and chive rolls

3 oz (90 g) white fish such as sea bream (whiting), cut into paper-thin slices

8 stalks fresh chives

Cut chives into 1 inch (2.5 cm) lengths.

Wrap each slice of fish around 4 or 5 chive lengths.

Add to a mixed sashimi plate. Serve with soy sauce and wasabi.

Makes 8 rolls

Above: White fish and chive rolls
Right: (Clockwise from left) White fish and chive rolls,
Sliced salmon, Sliced tuna, Squid, cucumber
and nori rolls, White fish rose

White-fish rose

You can make a rose using fish! Cut small, thin slices of white fish, such as silvery skinned mackerel or sea bream (whiting), sorigiri style (see page 34). (You can use tuna or salmon to make a rose.)

Roll one fish slice into a tight roll for center.

Add other pieces one at a time to make a rose. This may take some practice.

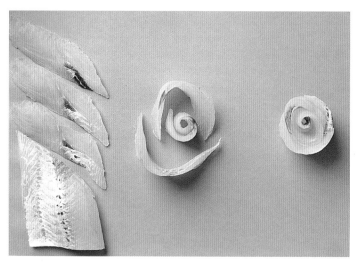

White-fish rose

Squid, nori and cucumber rolls

Squid, nori and cucumber rolls

7–8 oz (220–250 g) squid

2 nori sheets

3 oz (90 g) cucumber

Cut squid into a sheet 2 x 4 x 1/4 inch (5 cm x 10 cm x 6 mm) thick. Use a knife to score squid at 1–2-inch (2.5–5-cm) intervals running along length of slice. This will help you to roll it smoothly.

Cut nori into 2–4-inch (5–10-cm) sheets.

Cut cucumber into 1/4 x 1/4 x 2-inch (6-mm x 6-mm x 5-cm) sticks.

Lay squid on board, scored-side down.

Lay nori on top, then place cucumber slice on top.

Roll up, then cut into 1/2-inch (12-mm) thick rounds.

Makes 8 rolls

Tuna and nori rolls

2 nori sheets, quartered

7–8 oz (220–250 g) tuna fillet or other fish

Cut tuna fillet into 1 x 1 x 3-inch (2.5 x 2.5 x 7.5-cm) logs.

Lay a nori sheet, shiny-side down, on a bamboo rolling mat.

Place 1 log tuna on top and roll up as per maki-zushi method (see pages 48–49).

Place tuna nori log on a cutting board and cut off 1/2-inch (1-cm) thick slices.

Note: Rolls of this style can also be made by rolling tuna in daikon then rolling avocado in tuna.

Makes 8 rolls

Right: (Clockwise from front) Tuna and nori rolls, Sliced tuna, Tuna and avocado rolls, Tuna and daikon rolls, Tuna rose

SASHIMI

Garnishes for sashimi

Decorate sashimi with leaves or leaf cutouts (see page 100), cucumber decorations, wasabi and mounds of finely shredded daikon radish or carrot.

Lemon also goes very well with most fish. Simply cut half slices or wedges of lemon and add to the sashimi display.

Garnishes for sashimi: (Clockwise from top left) Shiso leaf, Cucumber decoration, Carrot decorations, Shredded seaweed, Shredded daikon on a shisho leaf, Shredded carrot

Carrot decoration

Carrot decoration

1. Peel and cut carrot into workable-sized pieces about 1–1$^{1}/_{2}$ inches (2.5–4 cm) long. Use the center part of the carrot, not the pointed end.
2. Stand the carrot piece on end. Cut a strip of paper $^{1}/_{2}$ inch x 2 inch (12 mm x 5 cm) and fold as shown.
3. Place the folded paper on top of a carrot piece and use as a template to cut the carrot into a pentagon shape. Then cut into petals as shown.
4. Slice thinly and use to decorate sashimi, chirashi-zushi and soups.
5. As an alternative, you can use a metal cutter designed for the purpose.

Cucumber decoration

1. Cut a 2 x 1-inch (5 x 2.5-cm) rectangle of cucumber about $^1/_4$ inch (6 mm) thick. It should have skin on one side.
2. Cut an odd number of slices along the rectangle, each about $^1/_8$ inch (3 mm) wide and $1^1/_2$ inches (4 cm) long, leaving the final $^1/_2$ inch (12 mm) uncut.
3. Leaving the outermost slices, use your fingers to curl every second slice down into the base of the cucumber.

Daikon radish

For each serving, you will need a piece of daikon about 2 inches (5 cm) long. Peel and shred or finely slice, then soak in cold water until ready to use. Drain and squeeze out excess water, then place on plate in a mound shape.

Wasabi

Wasabi can be placed on the plate in a mound or shaped into a leaf—the vein pattern on top is made with a toothpick. When eating sashimi, do not add wasabi to the soy sauce. Just pick up a small amount of wasabi at the same time as you pick up the fish. This will keep all the flavors separate.

Cucumber decoration

Dipping sauces for sashimi

Generally, soy sauce is used as a dipping sauce for sashimi. You may also wish to make your own blends with soy sauce and aji-ponzu, or add spiciness with chili powders and ginger. Tosa soy sauce, a mildly sweet soy variation, is also used quite often with sashimi.

Tosa soy sauce

3 tablespoons soy sauce

3 tablespoons bonito flakes

1 tablespoon sake

$^1/_2$ teaspoon mirin (optional)

Put all ingredients in a small saucepan and bring to the boil, stirring constantly.

Strain through a fine sieve over a bowl. Allow to cool.

Steaming the rice

5 cups (2¹/₄ lb/1.1 kg) short-grain
   rice

5 cups (40 fl oz/1.25 L) water

1-inch (2.5-cm) square kombu, or
   reserved kombu from Number-One
   Dashi, see page 104 (optional)

¹/₂ cup (4 fl oz/125 ml) sake
   (optional)

The first step in making sushi is to prepare the rice. It is well worth buying an electric or gas rice maker, as it reduces the process of making rice to the simple press of a button.

The following method is for Japanese-style rice, to which a vinegar dressing is added to make sushi rice.

Put rice in a bowl that is at least twice the volume of rice and add cold water to near top of bowl. Stir rice briskly with your hands to remove any dirt. Cover rice with your hands as you carefully drain away cloudy water.

Repeat process twice more. By third time, water should be clear. (Avoid washing rice too many times, as it removes starch and nourishment from rice and also breaks grains.)

Place rice in a colander to drain. In summer, it will need about 30 minutes, in winter, 1 hour.

If using an electric rice maker, place rice and 5 cups (40 fl oz/1.25 L) water in the rice maker and turn on. Machine will cook rice and tell you when it is ready.

If using an electric or gas stove, place drained rice and water (plus kombu for additional flavor, if desired) in a heavy-bottomed saucepan and cover with a tight-fitting lid. Bring water to a boil over medium heat. To ensure that rice grains are properly cooked through, do not remove lid throughout entire cooking process.

When water boils, increase heat and boil for about 3 minutes. If the pot boils over, adjust heat.

Reduce heat to medium and boil for 5 minutes.

Reduce heat to low and boil for 5–10 minutes.

Remove from heat and remove lid (water should no longer be visible).

You may wish to follow the practice of some sushi bars and add sake to rice before removing it from heat. This makes rice puff up and adds flavor.

Place cheesecloth or clean kitchen towel over rice, put lid back on and let stand for 10–15 minutes to finish cooking. Remove kombu, if used.

See following pages for vinegar preparation and combining the rice and vinegar to finish the sushi rice.

Right: Cooking sushi rice in a rice maker

Preparing the vinegar

OSAKA STYLE VINEGAR DRESSING

$1/_2$ cup (4 fl oz/125 ml) sushi vinegar

1 teaspoon rock or sea salt

3 tablespoons superfine (caster) sugar

TOKYO STYLE VINEGAR DRESSING

$1/_2$ cup (4 fl oz/125 ml) sushi vinegar

1 teaspoon rock or sea salt

1 tablespoon superfine (caster) sugar

While rice is cooking, prepare vinegar dressing, using one of the sets of ingredients on the left.

Place vinegar and salt in an enamel saucepan and whisk constantly over low heat until salt dissolves.

Add sugar and whisk constantly to dissolve. Do not let mixture boil.

Remove pan from heat when the heat is uncomfortable for your hand.

If made ahead of time, keep dressing in a closed jar in the refrigerator.

To combine rice with vinegar dressing: Place hot rice in a wooden rice tub or a large, nonmetallic, flat-bottomed bowl.

Spread rice out evenly around tub using a rice paddle or a wooden spoon.

Stir rice to separate grains, slicing paddle across bowl rather than stirring.

Make some space in center of rice and slowly add vinegar dressing in center to distribute flavor evenly. (You may not need to use all of dressing. If you use too much, rice will become mushy.)

Continue lifting and mixing rice with paddle, using a slicing motion. Use a hand-held fan to cool rice. Mix, then fan, then turn rice over and fan again. (Your aim is to make rice slightly sticky, with grains separated and evenly flavored with vinegar dressing.)

Continue mixing and fanning until rice reaches body temperature, then stop. If you let it become colder than this, it will harden.

Put rice into a rice holder that has a lid and will keep it warm.

Spread a piece of damp cheesecloth or a damp kitchen towel over top of rice and put lid on. (If you need to turn rice that is cold on top and hot on the bottom, or that has become overly compressed, cover your hand with this cloth and then turn rice with your hand.)

Rice is now ready to be made into sushi. Do not refrigerate rice as it will become hard. Sushi rice will not keep for more than 1 day.

Makes about 8 cups

Add the sushi vinegar to the cooked rice

Mix vinegar into rice using paddle

Fan rice to cool as you stir

maki-zushi

Thin sushi rolls are a simple, easy-to-eat style of sushi that is gaining in popularity as a light lunchtime food. They are made by wrapping sushi rice and ingredients in nori seaweed and shaping the rolls with a bamboo rolling mat. Usually only one type of filling is used, as the resulting roll is quite slender. With a little practice, thin sushi rolls are quite easy to make.

Keep some wasabi in a small dish alongside you so you can easily reach in with your fingers while you are holding other things. This applies to other small ingredients too, such as sesame seeds.

For making sushi rolls, a bamboo rolling mat is essential. If you try using a length of cloth or plastic wrap instead, the results are likely to be disappointing.

Sushi rolls should be eaten as soon as possible after they have been made. Nori soon absorbs moisture and becomes soggy, rather like paper.

The best-made sushi rolls have the filling in the center, with rice and nori in concentric circles around the filling.

Sushi rolls are always served with gari (pickled ginger slices) and individual bowls of soy sauce for dipping.

The type of garnish to serve will depend on the fillings that have been used and on personal taste. For example, white sesame seeds and shiso go particularly well with cucumber rolls.

Notes

Judge carefully the amount of rice and filling to place in the rolls. If the rolls are over-filled, the sheets of nori are likely to break.

If you want to add more ingredients, thus making a thicker roll, you will need to lay the nori sheet vertically on the rolling mat, giving you a larger area of nori to wrap around the ingredients.

It is best to serve rolls as soon as they are made, as the rice inside expands and the nori may split. The rolls will keep for up to 30 minutes if they are rolled in a paper towel and then plastic wrap.

Right: Tuna rolls (Tekkamaki) (See pages 48–9)

Tuna rolls (Tekkamaki)

5 nori sheets

2 cups (10 oz/315 g) Sushi Rice (see page 42)

Pinch wasabi paste

10 strips tuna, $1/4$ x $1/2$ x 3 inches
(6 mm x 12 mm x 7.5 cm), see page 34

In the old days, tekka were gambling dens where gangsters played traditional card games. When they got take-out sushi, the rice stuck to their fingers and the cards and made it easy to mark cards and cheat! So they suggested wrapping nori seaweed around the sushi rice so they could eat it without sticky fingers. This was a bit bland, so they added tuna.

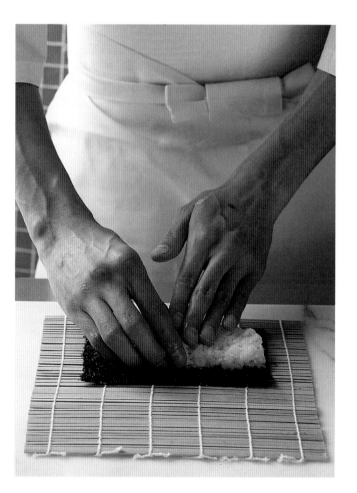

Take one nori sheet. Cut in half lengthwise, then cut $3/4$ inch (2 cm) from bottom of each sheet. You should have 2 sheets, each about 4 x $6^1/2$ inches (10 x 16.5 cm). (Scraps can be used for nori belts; see page 76.) Repeat to cut remaining nori sheets.

Place a nori sheet lengthwise on a bamboo rolling mat, shiny-side down.

Position nori sheet about 1 inch (2.5 cm) from edge of mat closest to you, and leave some space on each side of nori sheet.

Wet your hands and take a golf ball – sized handful of sushi rice. Gently squeeze rice into an oblong ball and put on center left of nori sheet. Then use your fingers to squeeze rice into a log along center of nori.

Makes 10 rolls (60 pieces)

1. Spread rice evenly over nori, working from left to right, leaving a $3/4$-inch (2-cm) strip of nori on far side uncovered.

Build a low ridge of rice in front of this nori strip. This will keep the filling in place.

Take a dab of wasabi on your finger and wipe from left to right across center of rice (if you hold your finger at an angle to start and flatten it out at end, wasabi will spread evenly).

2. Place tuna strips along center of rice, over wasabi.

3. Place fingers flat over tuna strips to hold them in place, then use your thumbs to lift up edge of bamboo rolling mat closest to you.

4. Roll rolling mat away from you, pressing tuna in to keep roll firm. Lift rolling mat over slowly until it covers rice and near side and far sides of rice join at ridge, but you still have a 3/4-inch (2-cm) strip of nori rice-free.

Covering roll (but not rice-free strip of nori), hold rolling mat in position and press all around to make the roll firm. Use your index fingers on top and fingers and thumbs on side to press roll together gently.

5. Lift up top of rolling mat and turn roll over a little more so that strip of nori on far side joins other edge of nori to seal roll. Use your fingers to make sure roll is properly closed.

6. Roll entire roll once more, exerting gentle pressure.

7. Slice roll in half, then cut both rolls twice to give 6 equal-sized pieces. Repeat with remaining nori and rice.

Cucumber rolls

5 sheets nori

2 cups (10 oz/315 g) Sushi Rice (see page 42)

3 cucumbers, cut into $1/_4$ x $1/_2$ x 3-inch
(6-mm x 12-mm x 7.5-cm) strips

2 teaspoons white sesame seeds

Prepare rolls in same way as Tuna Rolls (see page 48). Cucumber takes the place of the tuna, and white sesame seeds are added. Sprinkle sesame seeds along center of the rice before putting cucumber in place.

Makes 10 rolls (60 pieces)

Tuna and cucumber rolls

5 sheets nori

2 cups (10 oz/315 g) Sushi Rice (see page 42)

10 strips tuna, $1/_4$ x $1/_2$ x 3 inches
(6 mm x 12 mm x 7.5 cm), see page 34

1–2 cucumbers, cut into $1/_4$ x $1/_2$ x 3-inch
(6-mm x 12-mm x 7.5-cm) strips

Prepare rolls in same way as Tuna Rolls (see page 48).

Makes 10 rolls (60 pieces)

Right: Tuna and cucumber rolls

Salmon rolls

5 sheets nori

2 cups (10 oz/315 g) Sushi Rice (see page 42)

10 strips salmon, $\frac{1}{4}$ x $\frac{1}{2}$ x 3 inches

  (6 mm x 12 mm x 7.5 cm), see page 34

Prepare rolls in same way as Tuna Rolls (see page 48). If you wish, you can mince the salmon instead of cutting it into strips.

Makes 10 rolls (60 pieces)

Umeboshi plum rolls

2 sheets nori

1 cup (5 oz/155 g) Sushi Rice (see page 42)

20 umeboshi plums, pitted and chopped,

  or 6 tablespoons umeboshi paste

5 shiso leaves, finely chopped

Prepare rolls in same way as Tuna Rolls (see page 48). If you use umeboshi paste, apply it in the way described for wasabi paste.

Makes 4 rolls (24 pieces)

Natto rolls

2 sheets nori

1 cup (5 oz/155 g) Sushi Rice (see page 42)

6 tablespoons natto (fermented soybeans)

5 shiso leaves, finely chopped

Pinch bonito flakes

Prepare rolls in same way as Tuna Rolls (see page 48).

Makes 4 rolls (24 pieces)

Right: Natto rolls

THIN SUSHI ROLLS

futomaki-zushi

Thick rolls can be rolled in a variety of ways to make decorative patterns in the rice. Experiment in the way you lay out the ingredients and see the differing patterns that result. It is best to serve rolls immediately they are made as the rice inside expands and the nori tends to split. The rolls will keep for up to half an hour before serving if they are rolled in paper towel and then plastic wrap.

California rolls

4 nori sheets

3 cups (15 oz/470 g) Sushi Rice (see page 42)

8 teaspoons ocean trout or flying fish roe

1–2 cucumbers, cut into thin, lengthwise slices

8 jumbo shrimp (king prawns), cooked, shelled, veins and tails removed (see method and Note, page 74)

1–2 avocados, peeled, pitted and sliced

4–8 lettuce leaves, torn or sliced (optional)

California rolls, as their name suggests, were invented in California, although thick sushi rolls originated in the Osaka area.

See the step-by-step instructions on the following pages on how to assemble thick sushi rolls.

Makes 4 rolls (32 pieces)

Right: California rolls

1. Lay 1 nori sheet on a rolling mat and put ³/4 cup (4 oz/125 g) sushi rice on it. Spread rice over nori sheet, leaving ³/4 inch (2 cm) of bare nori at far side and making a small ledge of rice in front of this bare strip.

2. Spoon 2 teaspoons roe along center of rice, using back of a spoon to spread. Add lettuce if desired.

3. Lay 2 shrimp along center, with one-quarter of cucumber strips.

4. Lay one-quarter of avocado slices along center. Add one-quarter of lettuce.

5. Roll mat over once, away from you, pressing ingredients in to keep roll firm, leaving the 3/4-inch (2-cm) strip of nori rice-free.

6. Covering roll (but not rice-free strip of nori), hold rolling mat in position and press all around to make roll firm.

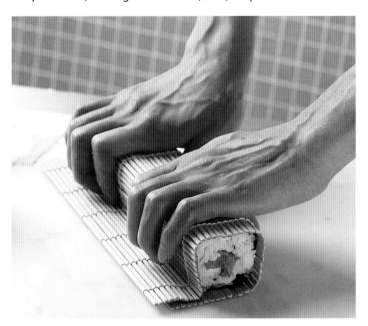

7. Lift up top of rolling mat and turn roll over a little more so that strip of nori on far side joins other edge of nori to seal roll. Use your fingers to make sure roll is properly closed.

8. Roll entire roll once more, and use finger pressure to shape roll in a circle, an oval, or a square.

Using a sharp knife, cut each roll in half, then cut each half in half again. Then cut each quarter in half crosswise to make a total of 8 equal-sized pieces. Cut gently to maintain shape.

Inside-out California rolls

4 nori sheets

3 cups (15 oz/470 g) Sushi Rice (see page 42)

8 teaspoons ocean trout or flying fish roe

1–2 cucumbers, cut into thin, lengthwise slices

1–2 avocados, peeled, pitted and sliced

8 jumbo shrimp (king prawns), cooked, shelled, veins and tails removed (see method and Note, page 74)

4–8 lettuce leaves, torn or sliced (optional)

This decorative style of sushi shows a chef's creativity. Having the roe on the outside of the roll results in the delightful effect of the roe popping as it touches your tongue.

See the step-by-step instructions on the following pages for how to assemble this style of thick sushi roll.

Makes 4 rolls (32 pieces)

1. Cover a rolling mat with a sheet of plastic wrap, folding it over edges and attaching it to back of mat. Turn mat over so plastic-covered side is facing down.

Lay 1 nori sheet on rolling mat. Use about $^3/_4$ cup (4 oz/125 g) rice to cover nori sheet, starting with a ball of rice at bottom and then spreading it out.

Cover nori with rice right up to edges.

Spread about 2 heaped teaspoons roe over rice, using back of a teaspoon.

Right: Inside-out California rolls

THICK SUSHI ROLLS

2. Pick up rice-covered nori by corners, quickly turn it over and place upside down on bamboo rolling mat.

3. Add lettuce, if desired. Place sliced cucumber along center of nori.

4. Add avocado, then shrimp.

5. With your hands held over base of mat and pressing in on ingredients with your fingers as you go, roll mat over ingredients, leaving 3/4 inch (2 cm) of nori visible at far end of nori end of roll.

6. Press gently to mold roll together. Lift up mat, roll back a little, then roll forward to join nori edges. Use gentle pressure to firm and mold completed roll into shape, either round, oval or square.

7. Using a sharp knife, cut each roll in half, then cut two halves in half again. Then cut four quarters in half to make 8 equal-sized pieces. Cut gently to maintain shape.

Futomaki with kampyo, omelette, soboro and cucumber

4 nori sheets

3 cups (15 oz/470 g) Sushi Rice (see page 42)

2 oz (60 g) Seasoned Kampyo (see page 96)

1–2 cucumbers, cut into thin slices lengthwise

Shredded thin 3-egg omelette (see Note, page 76)

Seasoned Shiitake Mushrooms (see page 96)

Shredded watercress, parsley or spinach leaves;
  bamboo shoots; soboro (optional)

To make, follow steps for making California Rolls (see page 54).

Makes 4 rolls (32 pieces)

**Right: Futomaki with kampyo, omelette,
soboro and cucumber**

Design futomaki

Just as you can experiment with different fillings in sushi, you can also use fillings to create strikingly decorative sushi rolls. You may like to use food coloring to dye the rice. The way you lay the ingredients out on the flat nori sheets and rice will affect the final design of your roll. Try putting all the ingredients together in the center. Laying ingredients flat along the rice gives a whirlpool effect to the final roll.

In the picture at the left, the sushi rolls have been made using colorful dyed rice wrapped in seaweed and then rolled again to make one large roll around an omelette. The square shape is achieved by pressing in the bamboo mat to make a square rather than a flat roll.

Right: Thick sushi roll wrapped in nori and thin omelette

THICK SUSHI ROLLS

temaki-zushi

Temaki-zushi are the easiest type of sushi to make at home. They are do-it-yourself hand-rolled cones of nori filled with sushi rice and a variety of other ingredients. They make excellent party food. Simply prepare the fillings ahead of time and lay them out attractively in separate bowls or on one large platter on the table. Give your guests a little guidance on how to make the rolls and then let them make their own, encouraging them to experiment with combinations of fillings. You may also wish to provide each of your guests with a hand towel. Japanese restaurants provide clean, damp hand towels for diners to wipe their hands on. (You can heat them in the microwave and roll them up like cigars for a truly authentic experience.)

See the following pages for ingredient combinations and suggestions, and step-by-step instructions on how to assemble sushi rolls.

Right: California roll–style temaki-zushi (left), Unagi eel and cucumber temaki-zushi (right)
Left: Tuna and shiso temaki-zushi (left), Prawn tempura and lettuce temaki-zushi (right)

California-roll-style temaki-zushi

5 cups (25 oz/780 g) Sushi Rice (see page 42)

20 nori sheets, halved

Wasabi paste

FILLINGS OF CHOICE

Salmon or tuna, minced or cut into $^3/_8$ x $^3/_8$ x 3-inch
   (1 x 1 x 7.5-cm) sticks

Jumbo shrimp (king prawns), cooked, shelled, veins and tails removed
   (see method and Note, page 74)

Unagi eel fillets, cut into $^3/_8$ x $^3/_8$ x 3-inch (1 x 1 x 7.5-cm) sticks

Sea urchin or salmon roe

Cooked or smoked fish, cut into $^3/_8$ x $^3/_8$ x 3-inch
   (1 x 1 x 7.5-cm) sticks

Omelette, cut into 3-inch-long (7.5-cm) strips

Cucumbers, cut into 3-inch (7.5-cm) lengths, then finely sliced lengthwise

Avocado slices

Sliced or torn lettuce leaves

Blanched vegetables such as asparagus, snow peas (mange-touts), sliced
   onion and carrot

White sesame seeds

Scallions (shallots/spring onions) or chives, finely sliced

SIDE DISHES

Gari (pickled ginger slices)

Soy sauce

Wasabi paste

Mayonnaise (or mix a little wasabi and lemon juice with mayonnaise to make
   wasabi mayonnaise)

Serve with individual bowls of side dishes, soy sauce and gari (pickled ginger slices), and rice.

Form the sushi rice into balls the size of Ping-Pong balls, or simply serve it in a bowl, along with a spoon for serving. Keep the spoon in a small container of water so the rice does not stick to it.

Note

A particularly effective combination of ingredients for temaki-zushi are those used to make California rolls (see page 54), namely ocean trout or flying fish roe, cucumber, avocado and cooked jumbo shrimp.

1. Pick up a sheet of nori and hold it flat in your left hand, rough-side up. Take a spoonful of rice and place an oblong ball of rice on left side of nori. Flatten out rice and make a groove for other ingredients. With a small spoon, wipe a little wasabi along rice.

2. Add filling or fillings of choice. Here we are adding long slices of cucumber and eel.

3. Fold near corner of nori sheet over filling to make a pointed end.

4. Use fingers to roll nori into a cone shape. Grasp nori to seal roll.

Nigiri-zushi is the type of sushi most often made in sushi bars. In Japanese, *nigiri* means "squeeze." Nigiri-zushi are made by gently squeezing together bite-sized pieces of fish (or other foods) and small balls of sushi rice.

At sushi bars, you may notice that sushi vary somewhat from chef to chef. The quantities of rice, wasabi and other ingredients differ a little, and the shapes of the rice and the topping may also differ. The shapes may be dictated by tradition, the chef's cooking style or the ingredients being used.

As your guide to size, remember that sushi is best eaten in a single mouthful, so for each piece use a ball of rice the size of a golf ball and enough topping to cover it. Use a moderate amount of wasabi for richer, more oily fish such as tuna and salmon, and less for mild-tasting seafood such as shrimp, squid and octopus.

In Tokyo-style sushi, there are two shapes used: funa-gata, where the bottom of the rice is convex, like the hull of a ship, and ji-gami no kata, or fan-shaped, where the bottom of the rice is concave. There are other traditional shapes, but they are not widely used. The important thing for the home cook is to make sushi that stand up and stick together well.

There are three or four commonly used methods for making nigiri-zushi. You may find that your sushi chef uses a different method, but we recommend the tategaeshi style, shown on the following pages, as it gives professional results and, with a little practice, is easy to master.

When making sushi, hold your hands comfortably at the level of the top of your stomach, with your elbows just a little in front of your body. Don't hold your hands too far away from you or too close in. Also, always make sure that your hands are a little moist, so that the rice does not stick to them. Have a damp cloth alongside for wiping knives, and a bowl of tezu (water mixed with vinegar), for keeping your hands moist. (The proportions are 1 cup water (8 fl oz/250 ml) to 1 cup (8 fl oz/ 250 ml) sushi vinegar.)

You may notice that your sushi chef has beautifully smooth hands. Both the oils from the fish and the acidity of the sushi vinegar in the tezu combine to moisturize and renew the skin.

Once you have mastered the method shown here, and tried the various examples provided, you can use your skills to create your own sushi.

Unagi eel sushi

In Japan, there are two ways of slicing unagi eels before skinning them to make sushi. Tokyo chefs cut from the back side. Traditionally, their samurai sensitivities were troubled by cutting from the belly side because it was seen as bad luck. The more practical merchant people of Osaka and its surroundings slice from the belly side.

Fresh eel is hard to find outside Japan. Much of the eel caught in other countries is exported to Japan. You can buy precooked unagi eel in frozen form in Japanese supermarkets. Simply thread it on skewers and grill quickly. Baste with sweet soy sauce (see page 87). Garnish with white sesame seeds, wasabi and sweet soy sauce.

Make eel into sushi using the nigiri-zushi method (see page 72). You may also use a nori belt (see page 76) to hold the eel in place.

Right: (Front) Garfish, Shrimp, Swordfish, Unagi eel with belt, (Back) Salmon, Squid with black sesame, Tuna, Sea bream (whiting), Bonito

Traditional method for making nigiri-zushi (Tategaeshi style)

Cut the slices of fish—such as tuna, salmon, sea bream, yellowtail, mackerel and snapper—just prior to making the sushi, using the sorigiri style (see page 34).

In order to make it easy to handle sushi rice and topping, prepare a bowl of tezu (half water, half sushi vinegar) and have it alongside you as you work. To wet your hands to the right extent, use your right index finger (if you are right-handed) to wipe tezu on left-hand palm in a circular motion, then clap your right fist over your left hand and wipe the water off your fingers so your hands are just moist. Also have beside you a small bowl of wasabi.

Easy at-home method: Use following method to form rice. Do not use slice of fish at first. When rice ball is well shaped, add fish. You will need a little pressure to join fish to rice ball.

1. With moist hands, pick up a piece of fish and hold it in your left hand hanging between thumb and index finger. Pick up a golf ball – sized ball of rice with your right hand.

Gently squeeze rice in your right hand to form a rectangular block with rounded edges and sides.

2. Lay fish piece flat in your left hand, across middle joints of your fingers.

Use your right-hand index finger to spread a dab of wasabi along length of fish.

3. Bringing your right hand over on top, place rice on top of fish.

Gently use your left thumb to press down on top of rice in middle, making a slight depression in rice.

4. Still holding your thumb to rice, turn your left hand over slowly and carefully from elbow.

5. With your right hand under your left, use your right-hand thumb and index finger to hold piece (along sides of rice).

6. Quickly turn your left hand over again so it is under your right hand (palm facing upwards) and place sushi piece back into your left hand (across middle joints of fingers).

With your right hand sideways (not above fish piece), use your right-hand index finger and thumb to hold and press sides of rice gently.

7–8. To form sushi, you will now use three actions together:
- Keeping your left hand relaxed and fingers slightly tilted down, your fingers will wrap upwards to hold and press sushi (which will then sit straight if you have tilted your hand down).
- Your left-hand thumb will hold and press end of log of rice.

- Hold your right-hand index and middle fingers straight and together and use them to gently press down along top of fish.

All these steps should be done in one quick, gentle pressing action, which is then gently released.

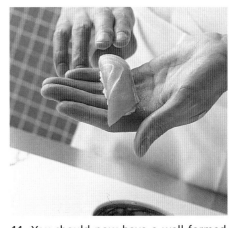

9. Hold your right hand over top of sushi piece and use your index and middle fingers on far side and your thumb on near side to pick up and turn sushi piece around in your left hand.

10. Repeat previous step, where you quickly pressed sushi with left thumb, left fingers and right-hand index and middle fingers.

11. You should now have a well-formed piece of sushi. If it is still not correctly formed, you may turn the piece around once more and press again.

Traditionally, as a final step, the chef uses his right-hand index finger to quickly wipe along top of fish, to make fish look shiny.

Preparing jumbo shrimp for nigiri-zushi

1.

2.

3.

This is the method to use when preparing jumbo shrimp (king prawns) for sushi. It will cook them the appropriate amount of time and prevent them from curling.

1. Wash shrimp under running water and cut off heads.

Insert a bamboo skewer or long toothpick along shrimp from head to tail, running along legs of shrimp without touching flesh.

Drop shrimp into a pot of salted, boiling water (use enough salt to make it taste like seawater). Boiling shrimp in salted water keeps protein in shrimp. They will sink to bottom and after 3 to 5 minutes will change color and rise to top. (Do not use a lid, or a strong smell of shrimp will remain.)

To check that they are cooked, remove one shrimp from water and squeeze gently. If inside is firm, it is cooked.

Quickly place shrimp in ice water. This gives them a good color and stops flesh from shrinking and becoming hard. When shrimp are cold, remove from ice water and place in a colander.

To remove skewer, use a screwing motion to avoid breaking flesh.

Remove shell from around body, but not tail.

2. To make butterfly cut, lay shrimp down with tail away from you, then cut from head to tail along belly with knife only going halfway in.

3. Use the knife or your fingers to open out and flatten shrimp carefully, without breaking the flesh.

Remove vein and rinse shrimp with mildly salted water. Lay on paper towels to drain.

Note: For sushi rolls and chirashi-zushi, remove tails and cut shrimp in half lengthwise, or leave whole.

Right: Jumbo shrimp nigiri-zushi

Omelette sushi

FOR OMELETTE

8 eggs

⅓ cup (3 fl oz/80 ml) Number-One Dashi
  (see page 104)

⅓ cup (3 oz/90 g) sugar

1 teaspoon mirin

Pinch salt

2 tablespoons light soy sauce

vegetable oil for cooking

1½ cups (8 oz/250 g) Sushi Rice (see page 42)

10 nori belts (see below)

Nori Belts

If you are using a topping that is prone to slide off the rice, such as omelette, scallops, squid, tofu or snow peas (mange-touts), you may need to use an obi-jime, or a nori belt, to tie the topping on.

After forming the nigiri-zushi, take a small strip of nori about ½ x 3 inches (12 mm x 7.5 cm) and use this as a belt to strap the topping firmly to the rice, as shown in the picture on the opposite page. This is called obi-jime-zushi.

1. In a bowl, beat eggs until just blended. Stir in dashi, sugar, mirin, salt and soy sauce. Heat 1–2 tablespoons oil in a square omelette pan over medium heat. Pour excess oil from pan into a bowl with a piece of greaseproof paper or cloth nearby ready to re-oil pan when needed.

2. Pour a thin layer of omelette mixture in pan. Use chopsticks or a spatula to press out any air bubbles.

3. When omelette is firm, run chopsticks around it to loosen. Using chopsticks, fold one-third of omelette from far side toward center, then fold this two-thirds over remaining one-third to the side closest to you.

4. Add more mixture, lifting cooked omelette up to let it flow underneath. When firm, fold over as before. Continue adding mixture, cooking until firm and folding.

5. Remove from heat and use a wooden board that fits inside the pan to press down and shape the omelette. Turn omelette onto a board. Allow to cool before using or refrigerating.

Without the right equipment, it may be difficult to create an omelette of the desired shape. Alternatively, cook omelette, lay it on a bamboo rolling mat and use the mat to flatten and shape it.

Cut omelette into strips 1 inch (2.5 cm) wide and 3 inches (7.5 cm) long. Make sushi using nigiri-zushi method (see page 72). Use nori belts to strap omelette pieces to sushi.

Makes 10 sushi

Shredded Thin Omelette: To make a thin, crepelike omelette to use shredded in chirashi-zushi or finely sliced in sushi rolls, follow Steps 1 and 2, then Step 5. Cut into fine shreds.

Right: Omelette sushi with nori belt

Battleship sushi (gunkan maki-zushi)

1 nori sheet

1 cup (5 oz/155 g) Sushi Rice (see page 42)

Wasabi paste

4 oz (125 g) sea urchin, salmon, ocean trout or
 flying fish roe

Some ingredients will not stay on top of rice unhelped, so with semi-liquid ingredients such as sea urchin and salmon roe, it is necessary to wrap the whole sushi within nori sheets to hold it together. When making gunkan-maki, remember that moist hands are good for touching the sushi rice, but it is best to have dry hands when handling nori.

Because nori is like paper, if you are making various kinds of sushi, leave the making of gunkan maki-sushi until last, otherwise the nori will become wet and may break.

Cut the nori into strips about 1 inch (2.5 cm) wide and 6 inches (15 cm) long.

Take a golf ball – sized ball of rice in your hand and gently squeeze it into a rectangular block with rounded edges. Place on a clean board. Repeat with remaining rice.

With one moist hand holding one rice ball, use dry fingers of your other hand to pick up nori sheet.

With rough side of nori facing rice, press end of nori to rice (it will stick) and then wrap nori all around rice. Gently press overlapping edge of nori to form a complete ring (or use a crushed grain of sticky rice to hold the ends together).

Dab a little wasabi on top of rice, then place roe on top of rice inside center of ring of nori.

Makes 8 sushi

**Right: Battleship sushi with ocean trout roe (left)
and sea urchin roe (right)**

Marinated mackerel (saba no sujime)

1 mackerel

Salt

Rice vinegar

This is a traditional style of sushi. The fish is marinated in a vinegar mixture and then used to make nigiri-zushi. Because it is already seasoned, you may not need as much soy sauce for dipping. Marinating fish adds to the variety in a mixed sushi plate.

Use the three-part method to fillet the mackerel (see page 30).

Wet some paper towels, squeeze out excess water and lay damp paper on bottom of a flat-bottomed container.

Sprinkle salt over paper and lay the mackerel fillets skin-side down on salted paper. Sprinkle salt over mackerel. Leave small fish for 2 hours, larger fish for 3 hours.

Remove fillets from container and gently rinse mackerel. Lay on clean, dry paper towel to drain.

Place fillets in a clean, flat-bottomed container. Pour rice vinegar in to cover fish.

Leave small fish for 30 minutes, larger fish for 1 hour. (If you prefer more fish flavor, leave fish in vinegar for a shorter time.)

Drain fillets, wrap in plastic wrap and refrigerate. Use fish the following day for sushi, making sure you have removed all bones.

Right: Marinated mackerel sushi

Japanese people always favor using foods that are in season for their cooking, and the variety of vegetables available through the year provides great scope for the imaginative sushi maker. Vegetables combine well with the delicate flavor of sushi rice, as do various other foods, such as omelettes, tofu and cream cheese.

If you are making a mixed platter of sushi, it is a good idea to make a few vegetable sushi to add color and nutritional value. You can experiment with cooked, blanched and raw vegetables and various garnishes.

Vegetables also offer an economical alternative to fish and seafood, which may sometimes be beyond the average household budget.

Experiment with garnishes such as fresh ginger, finely chopped shallots, miso paste and chili seasonings. You can also "Westernize" your sushi with your own variations.

Vegetable sushi often need to be wrapped with a nori belt to prevent the vegetables from falling off the sushi rice. You can use the scraps of nori from making sushi rolls or cut nori sheets into the appropriate lengths.

Tofu sushi

8 oz (125 g) firm tofu, drained

1 cup (5 oz/155 g) Sushi Rice (see page 42)

10 nori belts (see page 76)

Grated fresh ginger, minced scallions (shallots/spring onions), white or red miso paste, or mayonnaise, for garnish

Cut tofu into $1/4$ x 2 x $2^1/2$-inch (6-mm x 5-cm x 6-cm) pieces.

Make sushi using nigiri-zushi method (see page 72).

Wrap nori belts around sushi.

Add garnish of your choice.

Makes 10 sushi

Avocado sushi

1–2 avocados, peeled, pitted and sliced

10 nori belts (see page 76)

1 cup (5 oz/155 g) Sushi Rice (see page 42)

White or red miso paste, for garnish

Use 2 slices of avocado for each sushi piece.

Make sushi using nigiri-zushi method (see page 72).

Wrap nori belts around sushi.

Top each with a dab of miso paste.

Makes 10 sushi

Right: Avocado sushi with miso (left), Tofu sushi with freshly grated ginger and shallots (right)

Snow pea sushi

10 nori belts (see page 76)

1 cup (5 oz/155 g) Sushi Rice (see page 42)

20 snow peas (mange-touts), blanched and cooled

Umeboshi paste or mayonnaise for garnish

Make sushi using nigiri-zushi method (see page 72).

Wrap nori belts around sushi.

Garnish each with a dab of umeboshi paste or mayonnaise.

Makes 10 sushi

Asparagus sushi

10 asparagus spears, trimmed, blanched and dipped in ice water

10 nori belts (see page 76)

1 cup (5 oz/155 g) Sushi Rice (see page 42)

Mayonnaise and red chili seasoning (ichimi togarashi) for garnish

Cut asparagus spears 2–3 inches (5–7.5 cm) long and cut them into lengthwise slices if they are thick.

Make sushi using nigiri-zushi method (see page 72).

Wrap nori belts around sushi.

Garnish each with a dab of mayonnaise and a pinch of red chili seasoning.

Makes 10 sushi

Right: Asparagus sushi with mayonnaise and chili powder (left), Snow pea sushi with miso (right)

VEGETABLE SUSHI

Shiitake mushroom sushi

10 fresh shiitake mushrooms, stemmed

1 cup (5 oz/155 g) Sushi Rice (see page 42)

Rock or sea salt for sprinkling

2 lemons, cut into wedges

Using a sharp knife, score mushroom caps with an asterisk pattern, but avoid cutting through flesh.

Grill or broil mushrooms for 1–3 minutes, or until tender and darkened.

Sprinkle a little salt on mushroom caps.

Make sushi using nigiri-zushi method (see page 72), placing mushrooms either upside down or right-side up.

Serve with lemon wedges. Squeeze lemon juice on top before eating.

Makes 10 sushi

Eggplant sushi

1–2 Japanese eggplants (aubergines), peeled

Vegetable oil for deep-frying

1 cup (5 oz/155 g) Sushi Rice (see page 42)

White sesame seeds for garnish

SWEET SOY SAUCE

1/2 cup (4 fl oz/ 125 ml) soy sauce

2 tablespoons sugar

1 cup (8 fl oz/250 ml) mirin

Cut eggplant slices into 1/4 x 1 1/2 x 2 1/2-inch (6-mm x 4-cm x 6-cm) slices. Brush with oil.

Deep-fry eggplant for about 2 minutes, or until soft. Drain and cool.

Make sushi using nigiri-zushi method (see page 72).

Garnish with white sesame seeds and pour a little sweet soy sauce on top.

Makes 10 sushi

To make sweet soy sauce: Combine all ingredients in a saucepan. Boil to reduce to 1 cup (8 fl oz/250 ml) or 1/2 cup (4 fl oz/125 ml), depending on your taste.

Right: Shiitake mushroom sushi (left), Eggplant sushi (right)

Sushi chefs make many kinds of decorative sushi to celebrate special occasions. They use themes and motifs to suit the event, including flowers, fruits and animals; mythological and popular characters; and traditional, seasonal and religious items, all of which are created using sushi rice and other ingredients.

The sushi chef also uses his artistic skills to make beautiful centerpieces for sushi platters, all to add to the enjoyment of the dining experience.

The "apple" sushi on the facing page are made from minced salmon patted onto sushi rice balls, with a cucumber-skin "leaf" set on top. The "slice of watermelon" sushi is made from minced tuna patted onto sushi rice, dotted with black sesame for the seeds and with cucumber skin for the skin.

Here are two ideas for other new-style sushi.

Smoked salmon sushi crepes

Add minced smoked salmon and dried raisins to sushi rice and wrap in a crepe. Garnish with diced tomato, olive oil, salt, pepper and lemon juice. Place a mint leaf on top and serve.

Smoked eel and kimchee sushi in lettuce

Place sushi rice in a lettuce leaf. Put sliced smoked eel on rice. Top with chopped kimchee (Korean spicy cabbage). Wrap in a ball and serve.

Right: "Apple" sushi made from minced salmon around sushi rice, "Slice of watermelon" made from minced tuna on sushi rice, with cucumber skin

inari-zushi

Inari-zushi is named after the Japanese god of grains. According to myth, foxes are the messengers of Inari and guard the Inari shrines. Perhaps these sushi are so named because their pointed shape resembles the ears of a fox, or perhaps it is because foxes like deep-fried tofu.

Inari-zushi are a popular form of take-out food. They have a unique and intriguing flavor, the deep-fried tofu being both savory and sweet.

The basic technique for making inari-zushi can be adapted to make any number of variations. Slices of tofu that have been deep-fried are sliced open and used as pouches for sushi rice.

The deep-fried tofu slices are called abura-age-dofu. Do not try to prepare them yourself: you will need to obtain them from an Asian supermarket, already cooked. The type of tofu used to make abura-age-dofu differs from other tofu in that more coagulants have been used. It is sliced thinly, pressed to release moisture, then deep-fried twice. Before you use it, rinse it in boiling water to remove as much oil as possible. As well as being ideal for making pouches, deep-fried tofu can be cut up like ordinary tofu and used in miso soup, with simmered foods and in noodle dishes.

Deep-fried tofu slices are either square or oblong, and can be sliced in a number of ways to form pouches. Square slices can be sliced diagonally to make triangular inari-zushi. Oblong slices can be opened out by being cut down the two shorter sides and one long side, then rolled around a filling and tied with strings of cooked kampyo. If you open out a rectangular pouch and then fold the mouth inwards to about half the depth of the pouch, you can make inari that resemble little boats.

If you find it difficult to open the tofu bags, try rolling the sheets of abura-age with a rolling pin or slapping them between your hands.

As with most other types of sushi, the filling can be varied to suit your personal taste or to accommodate what is seasonally available. Some people add nothing to the sushi rice; others like to flavor it with sesame seeds that have been roasted golden brown, vinegared lotus root, hemp seed, Japanese prickly ash pepper (kinome or sansho) or lemon zest.

Whatever fillings you choose, they will need to be finely chopped or sliced if they are to fit comfortably within the tofu bag once they have been mixed with the sushi rice.

You may like to try these fillings:

- Sushi rice combined with finely chopped carrot, lotus root and cooked shiitake mushrooms
- Sushi rice combined with poppy seeds and finely chopped cucumber

Right: Simple inari-zushi

Simple inari-zushi

5 pieces 2 x 4-inch (5 x 10-cm) or 10 pieces
   2 x 2-inch (5 x 5-cm) thin deep-fried tofu
1 cup (8 fl oz/250 ml) Number-One Dashi
   (see page 104)
2 tablespoons superfine (caster) sugar
2 teaspoons sake
2 tablespoons dark soy sauce
1¹/₂ cups (8 oz/250 g) Sushi Rice (see page 42)

Place tofu squares in a saucepan of boiling water. Boil for 3 minutes to remove excess oil. Remove from water and drain.

Put tofu in a saucepan with dashi (use a drop-lid if you have one, a round wooden lid that sits inside pot on top of mixture and allows steam to escape around edges) and bring to a boil over high heat.

Reduce heat to low and simmer for 5 minutes. Add sugar and sake, and simmer for 5 minutes. Add soy sauce and simmer for 5 minutes.

Remove from heat, lift out tofu and drain.

1. Cut each piece of rectangular tofu in half to make 2 squares; cut square tofu diagonally to make 2 triangles.

2. Open center of each cut square or triangle to make a pouch.

   With moist hands, take a ball of sushi rice the size of a golf ball and gently squeeze it together.

3. Fill tofu pouch loosely with sushi rice. (If you fill the pouch too tightly, it will break.)

4. Wrap edges of pouch around rice to form inari-zushi.

Makes 10 sushi

1.

2.

3.

4.

chirashi-zushi

Chirashi-zushi is a great one-dish sushi meal that is easy to prepare at home. *Chirashi* means "scattered," and this is what you do: Fill a bowl with sushi rice and then scatter the ingredients decoratively over the rice. Almost any fish or vegetable can be used—it is up to the cook's imagination as to what it contains. Chirashi-zushi is usually served in beautiful lacquered bowls.

The following recipe uses mostly cooked ingredients, but chirashi-zushi is often made with sashimi. If sashimi are used, the dish is either accompanied with individual dishes of soy sauce, into which you dip the sashimi, or soy sauce is used to season the entire dish.

Chirashi-zushi often contains ingredients that are not used in other forms of sushi, such as kamaboko (fish cakes), baby corn, bamboo shoots, lotus root and soboro. Other ingredients that go well in chirashi-zushi are crab, avocado, carrot, green beans, bell peppers (capsicums), scallions (shallots/spring onions), unagi eel, squid, thick omelette slices, tofu, sardines and sesame seeds.

If you wish, you can season the sushi rice used for chirashi-zushi with chopped vegetables, green peas, chopped fresh ginger, gari (pickled ginger slices), soboro, crumbled nori, toasted sesame seeds, tofu or strips of deep-fried tofu, or various sauces. The dish is then known as bara-zushi.

Hint

If you use cooked ingredients, you can prepare chirashi-zushi in advance and use it as an "o-bento" food. (Bento is the traditional Japanese lunch box.)

Right: Sashimi chirashi-zushi

Chirashi-zushi

FOR SEASONED KAMPYO

³/₄ oz (20 g) kampyo strips

2 cups (16 fl oz/500 ml) Number-Two Dashi
   (see page 105)

¹/₄ cup (2 fl oz/60 ml) dark soy sauce

1 teaspoon superfine (caster) sugar

FOR SEASONED SHIITAKE MUSHROOMS

4 dried shiitake mushrooms, stemmed

¹/₂ cup (4 fl oz/125 ml) Number-Two Dashi

3 tablespoons light soy sauce

1 tablespoon superfine (caster) sugar

1 tablespoon mirin

1 cucumber

2 cups (10 oz/315 g) Sushi Rice (see page 42)

2 tablespoons shredded fresh ginger or gari (pickled
   ginger slices)

2 tablespoons soboro

2 tablespoons shredded nori

¹/₂ cup (2 oz/60 g) shredded thin omelette (see page 76)

4 jumbo shrimp (king prawns), cooked, shelled, veins
   and tails removed (see method and Note, page 74)

5–10 snow peas (mange-touts), blanched

¹/₂ unagi eel, grilled and cut into bite-sized pieces

Carrot and cucumber decorations (see page 40)

To prepare seasoned kampyo, soak kampyo in water for at least 2 hours, or if possible overnight. The longer the soaking, the better the texture.

Place kampyo and soaking water in a saucepan and boil until translucent and tender, about 10 minutes. Drain.

In a saucepan, mix together 1 cup (8 fl oz/250 ml) of dashi, soy sauce and sugar. Add kampyo to mixture and boil for 5 minutes. Drain and set aside to cool.

To prepare seasoned shiitake mushrooms, soak caps in luke-warm water for at least 2 hours or overnight. Drain, reserving liquid. Cut mushrooms into ¹/4-inch (6-mm) strips

In a saucepan, mix together remaining 2 cups (16 fl oz/500 ml) dashi, light soy sauce, sugar and mirin. Bring mixture to a boil, add mushrooms and simmer for 10 minutes. Remove from heat and drain mushrooms.

Cut cucumber crosswise into 2-inch (5-cm) pieces, then into thin, lengthwise slices.

In a large bowl or 4 individual bowls, spread out sushi rice to make a flat bed, keeping it loosely packed. Add following ingredients one by one, sprinkling them to cover the rice and then each other in layers: shredded ginger, kampyo, shiitake mushrooms, soboro, shredded nori and shredded omelette.

Make a decorative display on top with cucumber slices, shrimp, snow peas, eel and decorations.

Do not add soy sauce.

Right: Chirashi-zushi

CHIRASHI-ZUSHI

Suggested ingredients: for chirashi-zushi

- Toasted sesame seeds
- Deep-fried tofu (sliced and rinsed in boiling water to remove excess oil, then boiled in $\frac{1}{2}$ cup (4 fl oz/125 ml) Number-One Dashi (see page 106) and $\frac{1}{2}$ cup (4 fl oz/125 ml) water until soft)
- Tofu cakes
- Cucumber
- Avocado
- Cooked baby shrimp

Ingredients: (Clockwise from back left) carrot and cucumber decoration, shredded thin omelette, shredded nori seaweed, soboro

Ingredients: (Clockwise from back left) kampyo, jumbo shrimp and snow peas (mange-touts), ginger, shitake mushrooms

Adding ingredients to the chirashi-zushi rice bowl

1. Kampyo and ginger

2. Shiitake mushrooms and soboro

3. Shredded nori seaweed and shredded thin omelette

3. Jumbo shrimp and snowpeas (mange-touts), carrot and cucumber decoration

decorations

Traditionally, sushi and sashimi are decorated with bamboo and aspidistra leaves and leaf cutouts. These are used for both practical and artistic reasons.

Since the samurai age in Japan, bamboo leaves have been used for wrapping food and separating used in between foods. These leaves contain a sulfurous acid that kills bacteria. The leaves also keep foods from drying out and act as an insulating material. Bamboo and aspidistra leaves are now used interchangeably.

Camellia, ivy and cucumber leaves are also added as decorations to sushi and sashimi plates.

In Japan, there is a strong relationship between sushi and traditional bamboo leaf decorations. There are competitions to find the best cutting techniques to match specific sushi and the most creative cutting. Many of the younger generation of sushi chefs have not developed these cutting techniques. In many restaurants serving take-out sushi, plastic replicas of bamboo and aspidistra cutouts are used instead.

Draw your chosen design on the leaf and use a small, sharp pointed knife to cut it out.

Shikibaran, or shikizasa, cutouts resemble nets, and are put underneath sushi to prevent them from drying out.

The grasslike cutouts are placed in between pieces of sushi, like walls. They are named sekisho, after the borders between townships.

A kenzasa cutout resembles a sword (*ken* means "sword").

Kenshozasa are extremely difficult cutouts to make and need a good deal of practice. Illustrated here are two turtle designs and a crane.

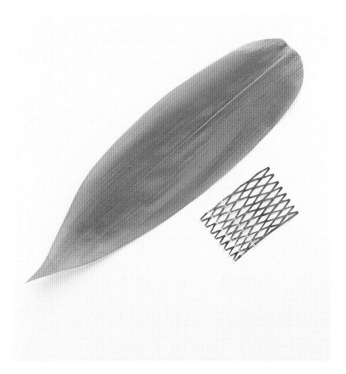

Bamboo leaf and a shikibaran or shikizasa

Varieties of sekisho

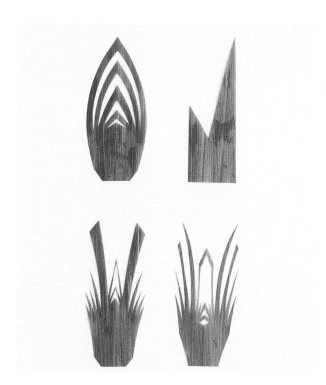

Varieties of kenzasa

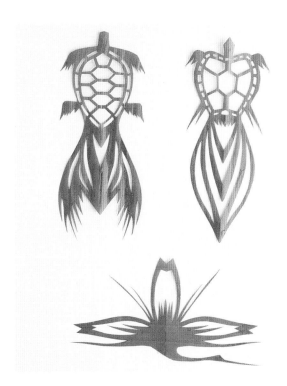

Three kenshozasa: two turtles and a crane

There are two basic soups served with Japanese meals. One is the well-known miso, the other is a clear soup called suimono. To make both, begin with a stock called dashi. Dashi is also the basic ingredient in many other Japanese soups, sauces and traditional dishes and can be used as a substitute for Western-style stocks and consommés. It has a delicate, mildly fishy flavor. Traditional dashi is made with bonito fish that has been smoked, dried and fermented for several months. The hard bonito is shaved into flakes on a wooden block and simmered in water with a piece of kombu, or dried kelp. People generally use already prepared bonito flakes these days.

We recommend making your own dashi using the traditional methods and ingredients because of the quality of the final stock, but as bonito flakes are not cheap and making dashi takes time, instant dashi (hon dashi) may be substituted.

There are two forms of dashi. Number-one dashi is stronger and is used as the base for clear soup. Number-two dashi uses the leftover ingredients from number-one dashi, combined with water to make a more diluted stock. This is then mixed with miso paste to make miso soup.

The miso paste you use and other ingredients you add will determine the strength of the soup's flavor. Lighter-colored miso pastes generally have a subtle, slightly sweet flavor, whereas the darker, or "red," miso pastes have a saltier, stronger flavor. Experiment with different miso pastes in differing amounts until you find the style that suits you best.

Right: Miso soup with enoki mushrooms and shallots

Number-one dashi

4 1/2 cups (36 fl oz/1.1 L) water

One 4-inch (10-cm) square kombu

1/2 oz (15 g) bonito flakes

This dashi is used for suimono, a clear soup. It is best prepared on the day it is to be served, but it can be cooled, refrigerated and used the following day. You can vary the amounts of kombu and bonito flakes to taste.

For vegetarian dashi, omit bonito flakes and double quantity of kombu.

Suimono

Suimono, or clear soup, is a simple, subtle soup based on dashi. As with miso, many ingredients can be added, and the delicate flavors balance well with sushi. Cook the ingredients you wish to add to the suimono, then pour the suimono over the top. The ingredients are not cooked in the soup, so the soup remains clear.

2 1/3 cups (19 fl oz/580 ml) Number-One Dashi
  (see recipe, this page)

1 teaspoon soy sauce

1 teaspoon salt

1/2 teaspoon sake

Place dashi, soy sauce and salt in a saucepan over medium heat. Heat until almost boiling. Remove from heat and add sake.

Makes 2 1/3 cups (19 fl oz/580 ml) suimono

Use a clean, damp cloth to wipe off white film on surface of kombu. In a saucepan, combine water and kombu. Let soak for up to 2 hours, then place over high heat and bring to a simmer.

When stock begins to bubble slightly, after about 5 minutes, check center of kombu. If it is soft, remove kombu from saucepan and set aside. If it is hard, continue cooking for a few more minutes, then remove.

Let mixture come to boil, then stir. Skim off any bubbles or scum on surface.

Remove from heat and add a small amount of cold water to lower temperature before adding bonito flakes. (Boiling water makes them smell.)

Add bonito flakes to saucepan. Do not stir. Use chopsticks to press the flakes down gently to bottom of saucepan. Let rest for 3 minutes.

Lay a cheesecloth or a clean napkin over a colander and strain mixture into a large bowl to remove bonito flakes. Remove the drained bonito flakes and reserve.

If, after tasting the finished dashi, you wish to strengthen its flavor, return mixture to saucepan and simmer for another 5 minutes.

Makes 4 1/2 cups (36 fl oz/1.1 L) dashi

Number-two dashi

Reserved bonito flakes and kombu from
Number-One Dashi (see facing page)
4¹/₂ cups (36 fl oz/1.1 L) cold water

Put all ingredients in a saucepan. Bring to a boil over high heat and cook for 15 minutes. Remove from heat.

Lay a piece of cheesecloth or a clean napkin over a colander and strain mixture into a large bowl.

Remove drained bonito flakes. Dashi should be clear.

Makes 4¹/2 cups (36 fl oz/1.1 L) dashi

Miso soup

4 cups (1 qt/1 L) Number-Two Dashi (see page 105)

2 tablespoons (2 oz/60 g) miso paste

Traditionally, miso soup is made with number-two dashi. For a more flavorful miso, you can use number-one dashi (see page 104). If using number-one dashi, you may need less miso paste.

Miso should be made to taste. Adding more bonito flakes or instant dashi granules to the stock will create a stronger flavor.

Add almost any vegetable, meat or seafood to the soup, but be sparing with strongly flavored or particularly aromatic ingredients. The following are ideal: diced shallots, diced tofu, wakame seaweed, daikon radish, corn, scallops, clams, fish, finely sliced shiitake mushrooms, enoki mushrooms, okra, pork, bamboo shoots and asparagus.

If ingredients need cooking, cook them separately and then add to finished soup. Ingredients such as tofu, enoki mushrooms, shallots and seaweed do not need cooking; just place them in the serving bowls, pour the hot soup over and serve.

Bring dashi to a boil in a saucepan over medium heat.

Put miso paste into a strainer. Hold or place strainer over boiling dashi.

With back of a wooden spoon that fits well in strainer, rub miso so that you sieve it through strainer into boiling stock. Discard any grainy remainders in strainer.

Stir soup as it simmers gently. Check for taste. Remove from heat and serve.

Makes 4 cups (1 qt/1 L) miso soup

Right: Miso soup with wakame, tofu and scallions

Health benefits

Not only is sushi a delight to look at and delicious to eat, it is also extremely good for you. The ingredients are always the freshest possible and low in fat. The Japanese have one of the lowest levels of heart disease in the world.

Fish and seafood are highly nutritious and low in kilojoules. Just a small portion of fish supplies between one-third and half of the protein we require daily. Most fish and seafood are excellent sources of vitamin B12, which is essential for building and maintaining cells, and of iodine, which is needed for the thyroid gland to work effectively. Seafood such as shrimp and squid are high in cholesterol, so are best eaten only in small quantities by people who need to limit their cholesterol intake. It appears, however, that crab and oysters lower blood cholesterol.

Oily fish, such as tuna and salmon, are a rich source of omega-3 fatty acids, which are highly beneficial in the prevention of heart disease and stroke.

Rice is the main food for more than half the world's population. It is a good source of protein and carbohydrate and, because it is digested slowly, it releases energy gradually. It has the additional benefit of being gluten-free, so can be eaten by people who are wheat-intolerant.

Vinegar has antibacterial qualities and has long been used to preserve food. It also has an extensive history in certain cultures as a tonic. It is used an aid to digestion, prevents fatigue and lessens the risk of high blood pressure.

Nori seaweed is rich in vitamins and minerals, notably iodine, and helps to curb the formation of cholesterol deposits in the blood vessels.

Ginger and **wasabi**, like vinegar, have antibacterial properties. Ginger aids digestion and helps reinforce the body's defences against colds and flu. Wasabi is rich is vitamin C.

Soybeans, which are used to make tofu and fermented products such as soy sauce, miso and natto, are high in protein, magnesium, potassium and iron. Soy products also contain phytoestrogens that act in a similar way to oestrogen, one of the female hormones. Soybeans have been used successfully in the treatment of premenstrual and menopause problems. Soy sauce is high in salt and can also contain wheat, so should be avoided by people who have problems digesting gluten.

Vegetables are an excellent source of vitamins, minerals and fibre. In addition, it has been shown that there is a lower incidence of cancer in populations where a good quantity of fruit and vegetables are consumed. Plants contain compounds known as *phytochemicals*, which help protect the body from disease.

Index

Published in 1998 by Periplus Editions (HK) Ltd.,
with editorial offices at 153 Milk Street, Boston, Massachusetts 02109 and
130 Joo Seng Road, #06-01/03, Olivine Building, Singapore 368357

Library of Congress Cataloging-in-Publication Data is available.
ISBN 962-593-460-X

DISTRIBUTED BY

North America
Tuttle Publishing
Distribution Center
Airport Industrial Park
364 Innovation Drive
North Clarendon, VT 05759-9436
Tel: (802) 773-8930
Fax: (802) 773-6993

Japan & Korea
Tuttle Publishing
RK Building, 2nd Floor
2-13-10 Shimo-Meguro, Meguro-Ku
Tokyo 153 0064
Tel: (03) 5437-0171
Fax: (03) 5437-0755

Asia Pacific
Berkeley Books Pte Ltd
130 Joo Seng Road, #06-01/03,
Olivine Building, Singapore 368357
Tel: (65) 280 3320
Fax: (65) 280 6290

Set in Frutiger on QuarkXPress
Printed in Singapore

First Edition
06 05 04 03 02   13 12 11 10 9 8